Piano Interval Workbook

Activities, Sight Reading, and Songs to Help You Read Music with Confidence

By Craig Sale

CONTENTS:

ISBN 978-1-5400-5625-2

Copyright © 2019 by HAL LEONARD LLC
International Copyright Secured   All Rights Reserved

Visit Hal Leonard Online at
www.halleonard.com

Contact us:
Hal Leonard
7777 West Bluemound Road
Milwaukee, WI 53213
Email: info@halleonard.com

In Europe, contact:
Hal Leonard Europe Limited
42 Wigmore Street
Marylebone, London, W1U 2RN
Email: info@halleonardeurope.com

In Australia, contact:
Hal Leonard Australia Pty. Ltd.
4 Lentara Court
Cheltenham, Victoria, 3192 Australia
Email: info@halleonard.com.au

Unit 1: Intervals

Reading music by intervals is reading by relationships. The relationship or distance between two notes on the piano or on the musical staff is an **interval**. Reading by interval relationships is a very natural and musical way to read notes. Music is always moving ahead from one note to the next. In interval reading, you read with this same forward motion rather than identifying individual notes one at a time.

Exploring

Intervals are best seen using the white keys of the piano. Try this:

- With finger 2 of either hand, play a D.
- Now go to the right of that key and play the second key.
- Now play up another second key.
- Now go to the left and play down to the second key.

When you play from one white key to the neighboring second key, you are playing the interval of a second!

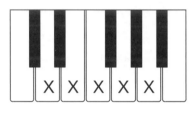

2nds

Now, try this:

- With finger 2 of either hand, play a D.
- Now *skip a key* going to the right and play up to the third key.
- Now play up another third (skip another key).

When you play from one white key to another white key while skipping one white key, you are playing the interval of a third!

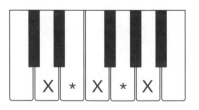

3rds

You can build bigger intervals by skipping more white keys:

- With finger 2 of either hand, play Middle C.
- Play up a 2nd to D.
- Play up a 3rd to F.
- Skip *two white keys* and play up a 4th to B.
- Skip *three white keys* and play up a 5th to F.
- Skip *four white keys* and play up a 6th to D.
- Play up a 7th to C. How many white keys did you skip? _____
- Play up an 8th (octave) to C. How many white keys did you skip? _____

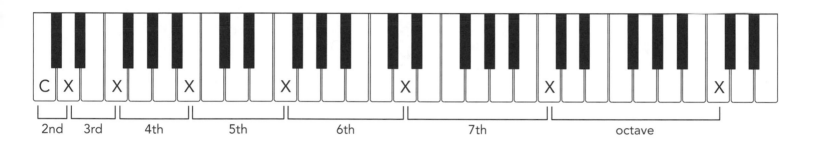

2nd   3rd   4th   5th   6th   7th   octave

Writing

Intervals can be seen on the musical staff as easily as on the white keys. Just think of each line or space as a white key. When you go from a line up or down to the neighboring space (or space to the neighboring line) you are going up or down a 2nd.

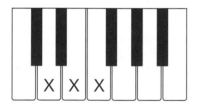

Just as 3rds skip one key on the keyboard, 3rds skip one space (or line) on the staff.

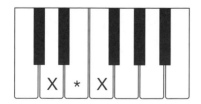
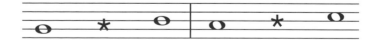

All the other intervals work the same way:

4ths

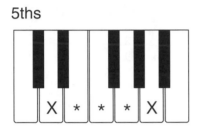 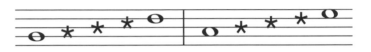

5ths

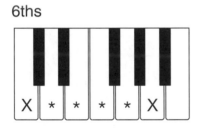 

6ths

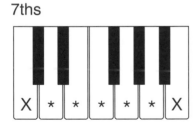 

7ths

Octaves

Playing

Intervals in music can be written and played two different ways:

melodic
(broken)

harmonic
(blocked)

Play 2nds through octaves, melodic and harmonic, with your LH (left hand) finger 2 on C and your RH (right hand) finger 2 playing the top note of each interval. Say "C up a 2nd, block," "C up a 3rd, block," etc. while you play.

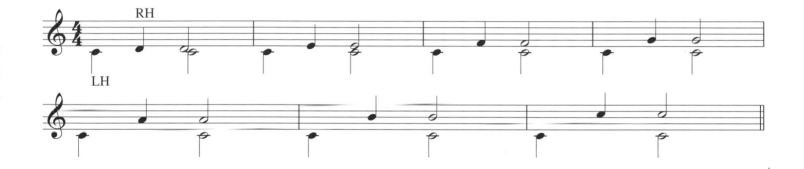

Reading bass clef, play 2nds through octaves, melodic and harmonic, with your RH staying on C and LH going down each interval.

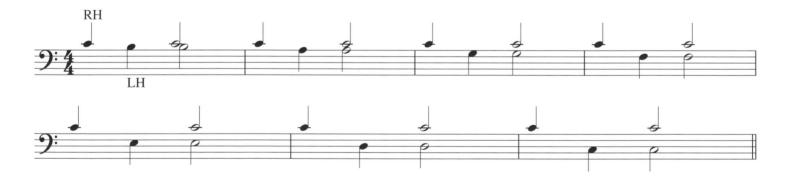

Creating

Now that you have seen how intervals work, explore the sounds of these intervals on your piano. Play melodic and harmonic intervals in high, low, and middle ranges of the piano. It can be fun to make your own music at the piano. Don't worry about writing it down—just explore and have fun! Try one of these ideas using intervals:

- Create a piece of your own that uses 2nds, 3rds, 4ths, 5ths, 6ths, 7ths, and octaves.
- Do you have a favorite interval? Create your own piece using just that interval.

Unit 2: 2nds

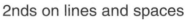

2nds on the keyboard

2nds on lines and spaces

The interval of a 2nd doesn't skip any white keys. It also doesn't skip any lines or spaces on the staff.

Exploring

Using finger 2 of either hand, play the following puzzles. Begin on the note indicated and use the same finger to play up and down 2nds as indicated by the arrow and interval. Write the name of the last note on the line. (Find the answers at the bottom of this page.)

1. F　↑2nd　↑2nd　↑2nd　↓2nd　↑2nd　↑2nd　_____

2. B　↓2nd　↓2nd　↑2nd　↓2nd　↓2nd　↓2nd　_____

3. D　↑2nd　↑2nd　↑2nd　↓2nd　↓2nd　↓2nd　_____

Circle the keyboards that show 2nds.

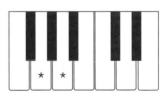

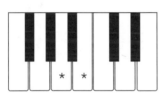

Draw an X **up** a 2nd from each named key on the keyboard.

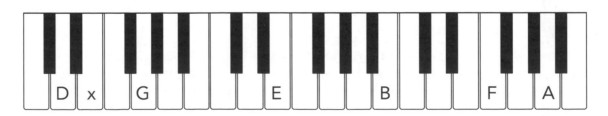

Draw an X **down** a 2nd from each named key on the keyboard.

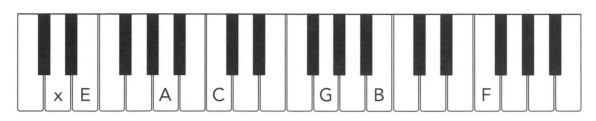

Writing

Circle the staves that show 2nds.

Draw the note **up** a 2nd from each of these notes.

  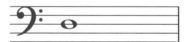

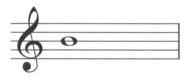  

Draw the note **down** a 2nd from each of these notes.

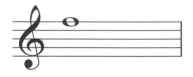  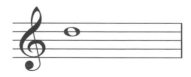

Draw the notes going up and down 2nds as indicated by the arrows.

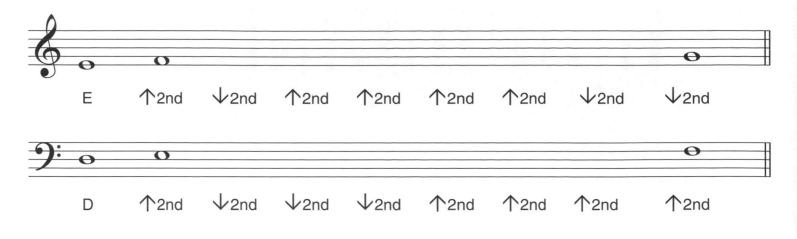

Playing

Just as 2nds don't skip white keys or lines or spaces, they don't skip fingers. Play this example using 2nds.

Solve these puzzles by playing 2nds from finger to finger. Play each puzzle first in your lap, then on the piano. Say the direction and interval ("up a 2nd," "down a 2nd," etc.) as indicated while you play. Write the name of the last note on the blank.

1. Begin with LH finger 2 on F: F   ↓2nd   ↓2nd   ↑2nd   ↓2nd   ↓2nd   _____

2. Begin with RH finger 3 on C: C   ↑2nd   ↑2nd   ↓2nd   ↓2nd   ↓2nd   _____

3. Begin with RH finger 4 on B: B   ↑2nd   ↓2nd   ↓2nd   ↓2nd   ↑2nd   ↑2nd   _____

4. Begin with LH finger 3 on E: E   ↑2nd   ↓2nd   ↑2nd   ↑2nd   ↓2nd   ↑2nd   _____

Reading

For each example, first place your hand in your lap or on the keyboard cover and play and say the direction and interval ("up a 2nd," "down a 2nd," etc.).

Next, find the position on the keyboard and play and say the intervals again.

1.

Creating

Explore the sound of 2nds (both melodic and harmonic) and make your own piece using 2nds.

Here is an idea to help you get started. Or just create your own!

Repertoire

Before practicing "Frére Jacques," study the intervals. Do you see any intervals in addition to 2nds? How many harmonic (blocked) 2nds do you see?

Frère Jacques

Cheerfully

French Folk Song

Unit 3: 5ths

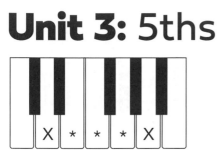

X * * * X

5th on the keyboard

5ths on lines and spaces

The interval of a 5th skips **three** white keys. On the staff, 5ths skip **three** lines/spaces (two spaces/one line, two lines/one space), and go from a line note to another line note (skipping one line) or from a space note to another space note (skipping one space).

Exploring

Using finger 2 of either hand, play the following puzzles. Begin on the note indicated and use the same finger to play up and down 5ths and 2nds as indicated by the arrow and interval. Write the name of the last note on the line.

1. C ↑5th ↑5th ↑2nd ↓2nd ↓5th _____

2. F ↓5th ↓2nd ↑5th ↓2nd ↓5th _____

3. A ↑2nd ↑5th ↑5th ↓2nd ↓5th ↑2nd ↓5th _____

Circle the keyboards that show 5ths.

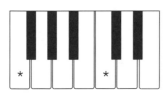

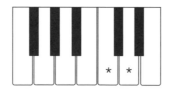

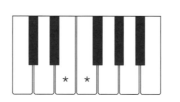

Draw an X **up** a 5th from each named key on the keyboard.

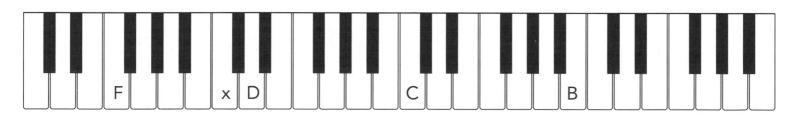

F   x D   C   B

Draw an X **down** a 5th from each named key on the keyboard.

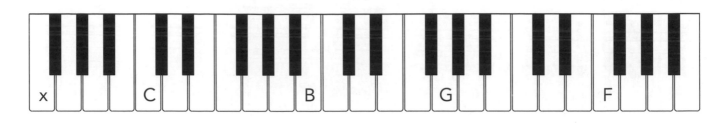

Writing

Circle the staves that show 5ths.

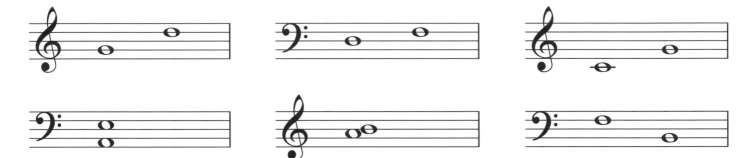

Draw the note **up** a 5th from each of these notes.

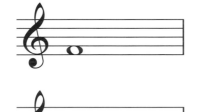

Draw the note **down** a 5th from each of these notes.

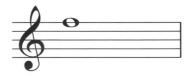

Draw the notes going up and down 2nds and 5ths as indicated by the arrows.

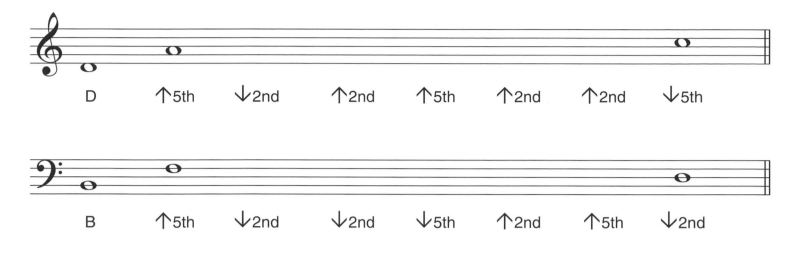

D ↑5th ↓2nd ↑2nd ↑5th ↑2nd ↑2nd ↓5th

B ↑5th ↓2nd ↓2nd ↓5th ↑2nd ↑5th ↓2nd

Playing

Just as 5ths skip **three** white keys and **three** lines/spaces, they skip **three** fingers. Play this example using melodic and harmonic 5ths.

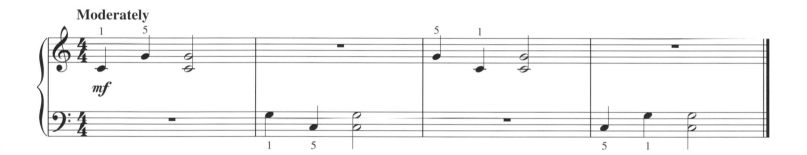

Solve these puzzles by playing 2nds (finger to finger) and 5ths (thumb to 5).
Play each puzzle first in your lap, then on the piano. Say the direction and name the interval ("up a 2nd," "down a 5th," etc.) as indicated while you play. Write the name of the last note on the blank.

1. Begin with LH finger 3 on C: C ↓2nd ↓2nd ↑5th ↓2nd ↑2nd _____

2. Begin with RH finger 2 on G: G ↓2nd ↑5th ↓5th ↑2nd ↑2nd ↓2nd _____

3. Begin with LH finger 5 on D: D ↑2nd ↓2nd ↑5th ↓5th ↑2nd ↑2nd ↓2nd _____

Reading

For each example, first place your hand in your lap or on the keyboard cover and play and say the direction and interval ("up a 5th," "down a 2nd," etc.).

Next, play the example on the keyboard and say the intervals again as you play.

1.

2.

3.

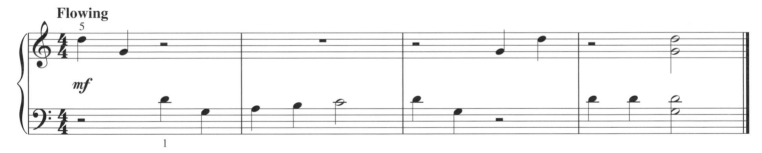

Creating

Explore the sound of 5ths (both melodic and harmonic) and make your own piece using 5ths. Here is an idea to help you get started. Or just create your own!

Repertoire

Before practicing this piece, study the intervals. Circle all the 5ths. Notice the suggested fingering for the first 5th in the right hand. Instead of playing the 5th with your thumb and finger 5, you will need to extend the hand to play the note up a 5th with finger 4.

Twinkle, Twinkle Little Star

French Folk Song

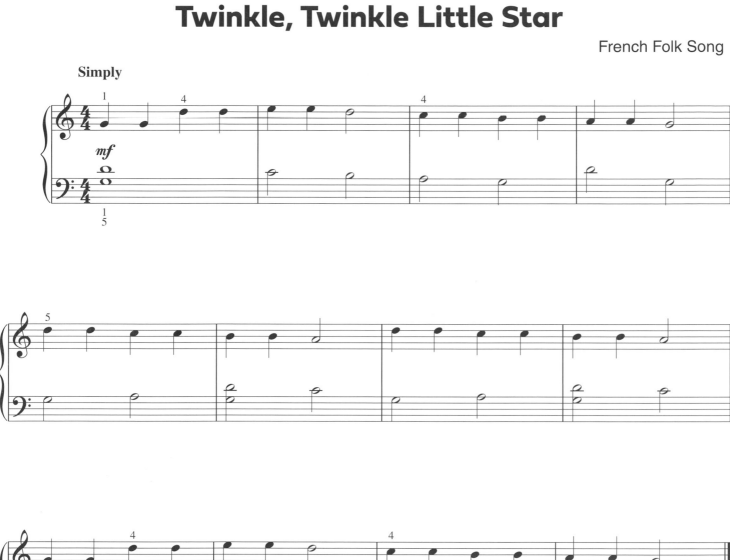

Unit 4: 3rds

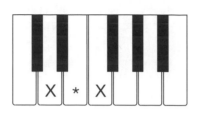

3rd on the keyboard

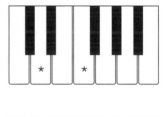

3rds on lines and spaces

The interval of a 3rd skips **one** white key. On the staff, 3rds skip **one** line or space, and go from a line note to another line note (skipping a space) or from a space note to another space note (skipping a line).

Exploring

Using finger 2 of either hand, play the following puzzles. Begin on the note indicated and use the same finger to play up and down as indicated by the arrow and interval. Write the name of the last note on the line.

1. G   ↑2nd   ↑3rd   ↑5th   ↓2nd   ↓3rd   _____

2. F   ↓2nd   ↓3rd   ↑3rd   ↑5th   ↓2nd   _____

3. D   ↑3rd   ↑3rd   ↓2nd   ↓5th   ↓5th   ↑2nd   ↑3rd   ↑2nd   _____

Circle the keyboards that show 3rds.

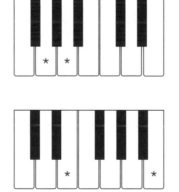

Draw an X **up** a 3rd from each named key on the keyboard.

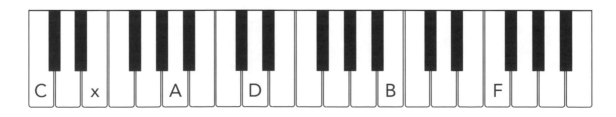

16

Draw an X **down** a 3rd from each named key on the keyboard.

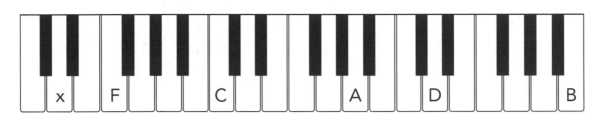

Writing

Circle the staves that show 3rds.

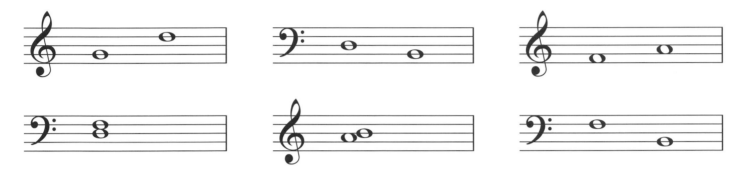

Draw the note **up** a 3rd from each of these notes.

Draw a blocked 3rd and then blocked 5th **above** each of these notes as shown in the first example.

Draw the note **down** a 3rd from each of these notes.

Draw a blocked 3rd and then blocked 5th **below** each of these notes.

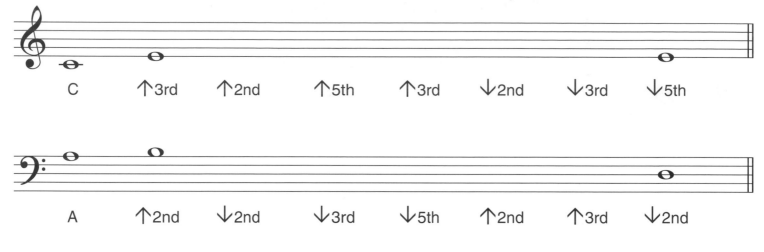

Draw the notes going up and down 2nds, 3rds, and 5ths as indicated by the arrows.

C   ↑3rd   ↑2nd   ↑5th   ↑3rd   ↓2nd   ↓3rd   ↓5th

A   ↑2nd   ↓2nd   ↓3rd   ↓5th   ↑2nd   ↑3rd   ↓2nd

Playing

Just as 3rds skip **one** white key and **one** line or space, they skip **one** finger. Play the following example using melodic and harmonic 3rds.

Solve these puzzles by playing 2nds (finger to finger), 5ths (thumb to 5), and 3rds (thumb to 3, 2 to 4, 3 to 5). Play each puzzle first in your lap or on the keyboard cover, then on the piano. Say the direction and interval ("up a 2nd, down a 3rd," etc.) as indicated while you play. Write the name of the last note in the blank.

1. Begin with RH finger 2 on D: D   ↓2nd   ↑3rd   ↑2nd   ↓3rd   ↓2nd   ↑5th   _____

2. Begin with LH finger 3 on G: G   ↓2nd   ↑3rd   ↓2nd   ↓3rd   ↑5th   ↓3rd   _____

3. Begin with RH thumb on F: F   ↑2nd   ↑3rd   ↓3rd   ↓2nd   ↑5th   ↓3rd   _____

Reading

For each example, first place your hand in your lap or on the keyboard cover and play and say the direction and interval ("up a 3rd," "down a 2nd," etc.).

Next, play the example on the keyboard and say the intervals again as you play.

1.

2.

3.

Creating

Explore the sound of 3rds (both melodic and harmonic) and make your own piece using 3rds. Here is an idea to help you get started. Or just create your own!

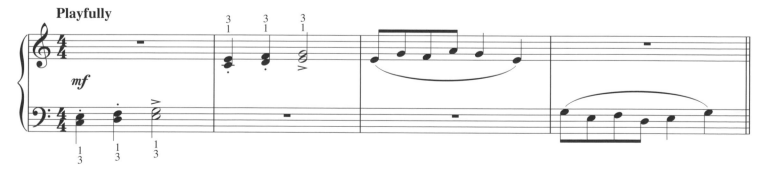

This famous piece by Beethoven uses lots of 3rds! Your right hand will move frequently. Use the fingering given to help you stretch and shift as needed. Practice these moves and look for repeated notes, 2nds, and 3rds.

Theme from Symphony No. 5

By Ludwig Van Beethoven

With drama

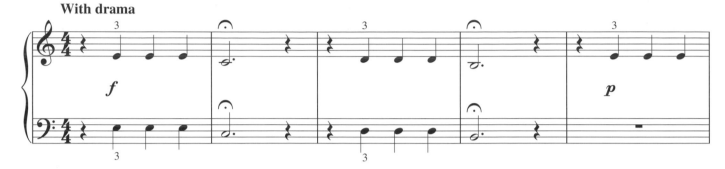

Unit 5: 4ths

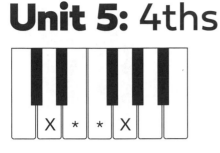

4th on the keyboard

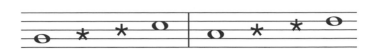

4ths on lines and spaces

The interval of a 4th skips **two** white keys. On the staff, 4ths skip **two** notes (one line and one space), and go from a line note to a space note or from a space note to line note.

Exploring

Using finger 2 of either hand, play the following puzzles. Begin on the note indicated and use the same finger to play up and down as indicated by the arrow and interval. Write the name of the last note on the line.

1. E ↑2nd ↑3rd ↑4th ↓2nd ↓4th ↓5th _____

2. A ↓2nd ↓4th ↓3rd ↑2nd ↑4th ↑4th _____

3. G ↑4th ↑3rd ↓2nd ↓4th ↓5th ↑2nd ↑2nd _____

Circle the keyboards that show 4ths.

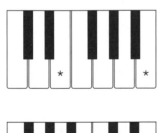

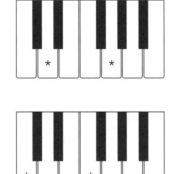

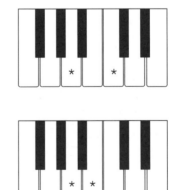

Draw an X **up** a 4th from each named key on the keyboard.

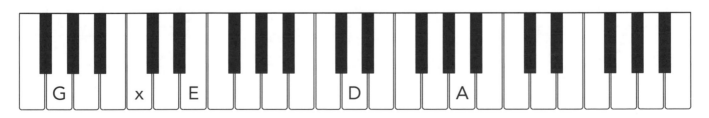

Draw an X **down** a 4th from each named key on the keyboard.

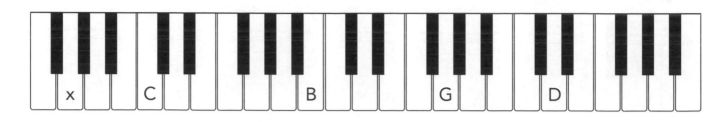

Writing

Circle the staves that show 4ths.

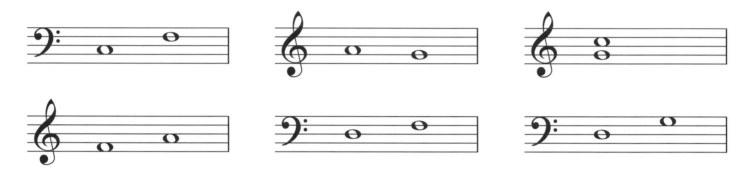

Draw the note **up** a 4th from each of these notes.

Draw a blocked 2nd and then blocked 4th **above** each of these notes.

Draw the note **down** a 4th from each of these notes.

Draw a blocked 2nd and then blocked 4th **below** each of these notes.

Draw the notes going up and down as indicated by the arrows and intervals.

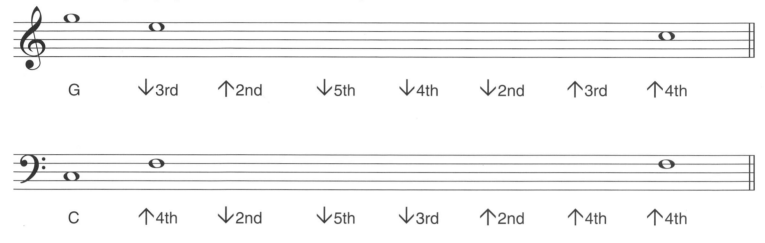

G   ↓3rd   ↑2nd   ↓5th   ↓4th   ↓2nd   ↑3rd   ↑4th

C   ↑4th   ↓2nd   ↓5th   ↓3rd   ↑2nd   ↑4th   ↑4th

Playing

Just as 4ths skip **two** white keys and **two** notes on the staff, they skip **two** fingers. Play this example using melodic and harmonic 4ths.

Solve these puzzles by playing 2nds, 3rds, 5ths, and 4ths (thumb to finger 4, finger 2 to finger 5). Play each puzzle first in your lap, then on the piano. Say the direction and interval as indicated while you play. Write the name of the last note in the blank.

1. Begin with LH thumb on G: G   ↓2   ↓4   ↑3   ↑3   ↓5   ↑4   _____

2. Begin with RH finger 2 on E: E   ↑4   ↓3   ↓2   ↑3   ↓2   ↓2   ↑4   _____

3. Begin with LH finger 3 on B: B   ↑2   ↓4   ↑5   ↓4   ↑2   ↑3   ↓4   _____

Reading

For each example, first place your hand in your lap or on the keyboard cover and play and say the direction and interval ("up a 3rd," "down a 4th," etc.).

Next, play the example on the keyboard and say the intervals again as you play.

1.

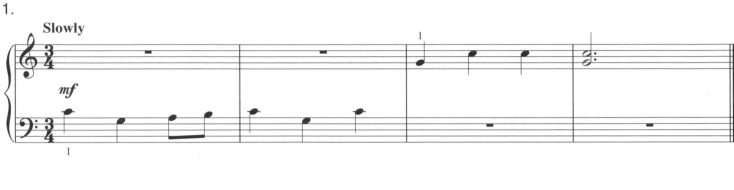

2.

3.

Creating

Explore the sound of 4ths (both melodic and harmonic) and make your own piece using 4ths. Here is an idea to help you get started. Or just create your own!

Repertoire

This song became popular during the American Civil War. In the 1950s, Elvis Presley used the tune for his hit "Love Me Tender."

Although this tune begins with the interval of a 4th, you will find lots of 2nds, 3rds, and 5ths too! Before practicing each hand, identify the intervals you are going to play. Listen for smooth, connected phrases, as indicated by the long slurs over the treble staff.

Aura Lee

American Folk Song

Unit 6: 2nds-5ths Review

Exploring

On the keyboard below:

Go **up** the designated interval from each X and write the name of that key.

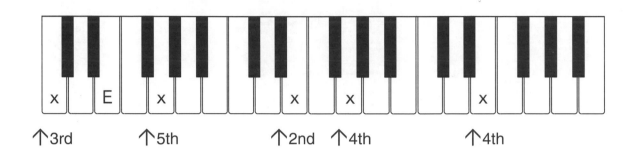

On the keyboard below:

Go **down** the designated interval from each X and write the name of that key.

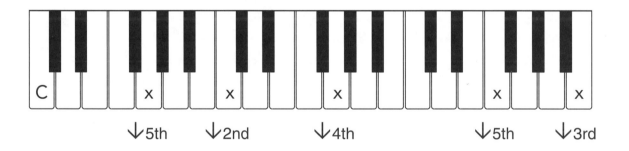

Use your mind to solve these interval puzzles—no fingers, no keys—just your brain!

1. THINK: C ↑5th ↑2nd ↓3rd ↓3rd ↓4th

What note did you imagine ending on? ____

2. THINK: G ↓2nd ↓3rd ↓2nd ↑5th ↑5th

What note did you imagine ending on? ____

3. THINK: B ↑3rd ↑3rd ↓2nd ↑4th ↓2nd ↓3rd

What note did you imagine ending on? ____

Writing

Draw the interval **above** each note as indicated. Then, write the name of the note you draw on the line.

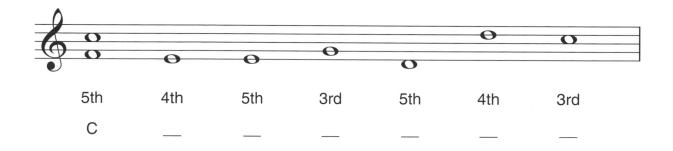

5th	4th	5th	3rd	5th	4th	3rd
C	—	—	—	—	—	—

Draw the interval **below** each note as indicated. Then, write the name of the note you draw on the line.

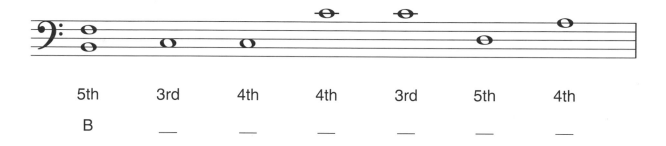

5th	3rd	4th	4th	3rd	5th	4th
B	—	—	—	—	—	—

Fill in the missing quarter notes as indicated by the arrow and interval. The last missing note is a whole note. Play the tune. Do you recognize it? Write the title on the line.

_____

Playing and Writing

Play and say the direction and intervals, reading the arrows and numbers.

Begin with RH 2 on F:

F ↓2nd ↑4th ↓3rd ↓2nd ↑5th

Now, play and say the direction and intervals written on the staff.

Did they sound the same? _____

Play and say the direction and intervals, then write the notes on the staff. Play what you have written to be sure they match!

1. Begin with RH finger 1 on G:

G ↑2nd ↑3rd ↓4th ↑5th ↓2nd

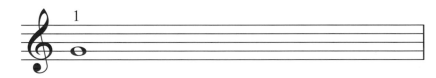

2. Begin with LH finger 2 on C:

C ↓4th ↑3rd ↓2nd ↑4th ↓5th

3. Begin with RH finger 3 on F:

F ↑3rd ↓5th ↑2nd ↑3rd ↓3rd

Creating

Here is a jumble of ideas for a piece using 2nds, 3rds, 4ths, and 5ths. Put them together in any way you like! Try them out in different orders. Some of them might sound good played at the same time. You might even want to build on these by adding your own ideas to the jumble!

2nds

5ths

3rds

4ths

This piece by Reinagle uses all of the intervals studied so far. Before practicing, study the intervals used in each hand. Then practice lines 1, 2, and 4: first hands separately, then hands together. You will see that after learning line 4, you already know line 3!

Allegro

By Alexander Reinagle

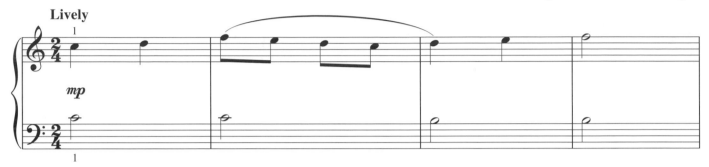

Unit 7: 6ths

6th on the keyboard

6ths on lines and spaces

The interval of a 6th skips **four** white keys. On the staff, 6ths skip **four** lines/spaces (two of each), and go from a line note to a space note or from a space note to a line note.

What other intervals go from a line to a space and a space to a line? _____ and _____

Exploring

Using finger 2 of either hand, play the following puzzles. Begin on the note indicated and use the same finger to play up and down as indicated by the arrow and interval. Write the name of the last note on the line.

1. C ↑2nd ↑3rd ↑4th ↑5th ↑6th ↓2nd ↓6th _____

2. F ↓2nd ↓6th ↑3rd ↑4th ↓2nd ↓6th ↑3rd _____

3. E ↑6th ↑6th ↓3rd ↑2nd ↑4th ↓2nd ↓5th _____

Circle the keyboards that show 6ths.

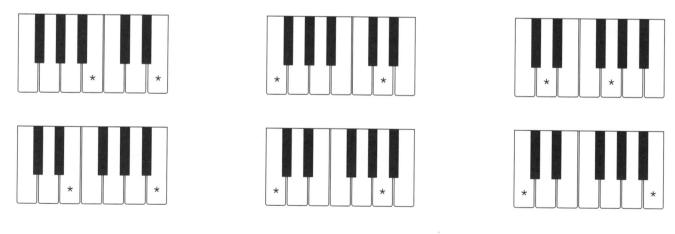

Draw an X **up** a 6th from each named key on the keyboard.

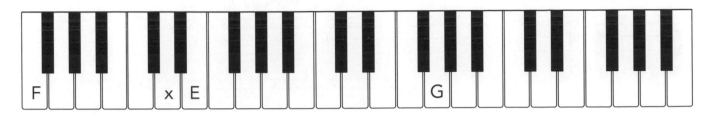

Draw an X **down** a 6th from each named key on the keyboard.

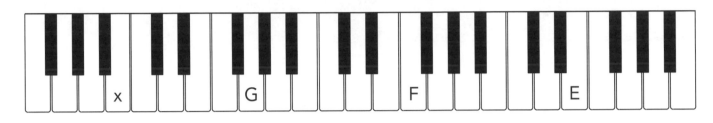

Writing

Circle the staves that show 6ths.

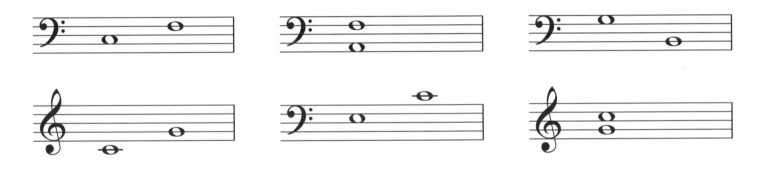

Draw the note **up** a 6th from each of these notes.

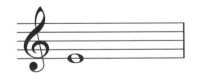

Draw the note **down** a 6th from each of these notes.

Draw the notes going up and down as indicated by the arrows and intervals.

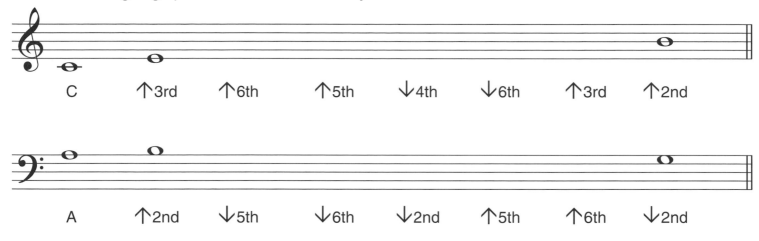

C ↑3rd ↑6th ↑5th ↓4th ↓6th ↑3rd ↑2nd

A ↑2nd ↓5th ↓6th ↓2nd ↑5th ↑6th ↓2nd

Playing

When playing 2nds through 5ths, your fingers were able to rest on five neighboring white keys. Playing 6ths requires you to reach beyond those five keys. Expanding between your thumb and finger 2 is the easiest and most natural way to do this.

When you play a 6th with RH, notice that finger 2 rests on the key a 3rd above the thumb.

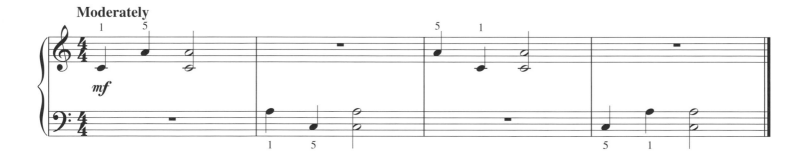

Play each puzzle first in your lap, then on the piano. Say the direction and interval as indicated while you play. Write the name of the last note in the blank.

1. Begin with LH thumb on F: F ↓6th ↑2nd ↑3rd ↓2nd ↓3rd ↑6th _____

2. Begin with RH thumb on G: G ↑6th ↓2nd ↓3rd ↓2nd ↑5th ↓6th _____

Reading

For each example, first place your hand in your lap or on the keyboard cover and play and say the direction and interval ("up a 6th," "down a 4th," etc.).

Next, play the example on the keyboard and say the intervals again as you play.

1.

2.

3.

Creating

Explore the sound of 6ths (both melodic and harmonic) and make your own piece using 6ths. Here is an idea to help you get started. Or just create your own!

This song features the interval of a 6th. Because this piece is written in the key of G Major, every F is played as F♯. Circle all of the Fs before you begin practicing this piece. Notice how the combinations of blocked intervals in line 3 create rich harmonies.

My Bonnie Lies Over the Ocean

Scottish Folk Song

Unit 8: 7ths

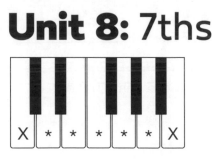

7th on the keyboard

7ths on lines and spaces

The interval of a 7th skips **five** white keys. On the staff, 7ths skip **five** lines/spaces (three spaces/two lines, three lines/two spaces), and go from a line note to another line note (skipping two lines) or from a space note to another space note (skipping two spaces).

What other intervals go from a line to a line and a space to a space? _____ and _____

Exploring

Using finger 2 of either hand, play the following puzzles. Begin on the note indicated and use the same finger to play up and down as indicated by the arrow and interval. Write the name of the last note on the line.

1. B ↑2nd ↑5th ↑6th ↑7th ↓2nd ↓7th ↓3rd _____

2. G ↑3rd ↓2nd ↑5th ↑7th ↓4th _____

3. E ↓2nd ↓7th ↑3rd ↑6th ↑2nd ↓3rd ↓2nd _____

Circle the keyboards that show 7ths.

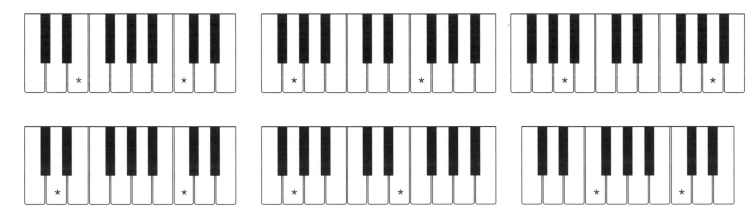

Draw an X **up** a 7th from each named key on the keyboard.

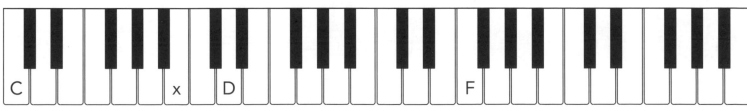

Draw an X **down** a 7th from each named key on the keyboard.

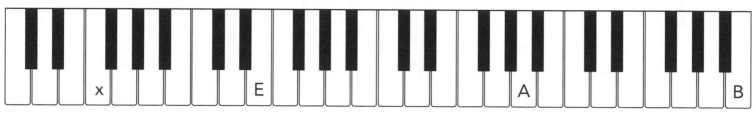

Writing

Circle the staves that show 7ths.

Draw the note **up** a 7th from each of these notes.

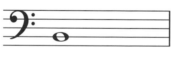

Draw the note **down** a 7th from each of these notes.

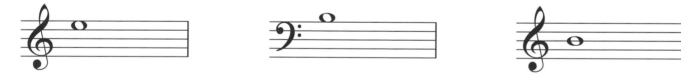

Draw the notes going up and down as indicated by the arrows and intervals.

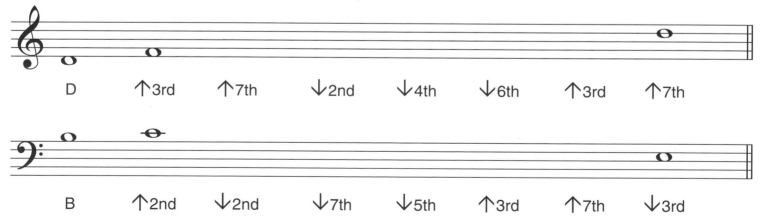

D   ↑3rd   ↑7th   ↓2nd   ↓4th   ↓6th   ↑3rd   ↑7th

B   ↑2nd   ↓2nd   ↓7th   ↓5th   ↑3rd   ↑7th   ↓3rd

Playing

Playing a 7th requires you to reach one note further than a 6th.

When you play a 7th, notice that finger 2 rests on the key a 4th above the thumb.

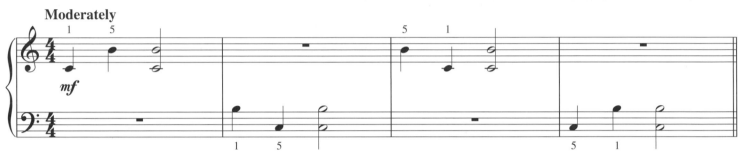

Play each puzzle first in your lap, then on the piano. Say the direction and interval as indicated while you play. Write the name of the last note in the blank.

1. Begin with RH finger 3 on E: E   ↓3rd   ↑7th   ↓2nd   ↓3rd   ↓2nd   ↑6th   _____

2. Begin with LH finger 4 on G: G   ↑4th   ↓7th   ↑2nd   ↓2nd   ↑5th   ↓6th   _____

Reading

For each example, first place your hand in your lap or on the keyboard cover and play and say the direction and interval ("up a 7th," "down a 4th," etc.).

Next, play the example on the keyboard and say the intervals again as you play.

1.

2.

3.

Creating your own piece

Explore the sound of 7ths and make your own piece. Here is an idea to help you get started. Or just create your own!

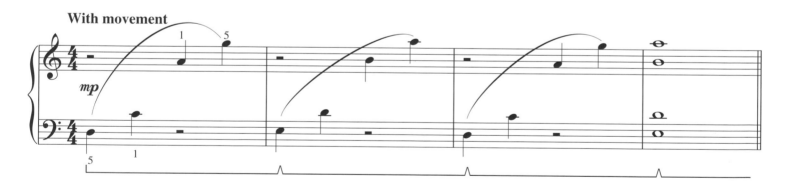

Repertoire

This piece uses every interval from 2nds through 7ths. Circle all the 7ths and draw a box around the 6ths. Practice the melody (RH lines 1 and 2, LH lines 3 and 4) alone and then the accompaniment (LH lines 1 and 2, RH lines 3 and 4) before playing both hands together.

Lullaby

By Craig Sale

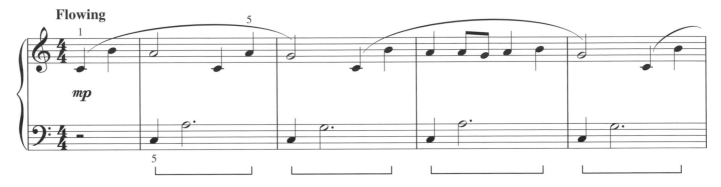

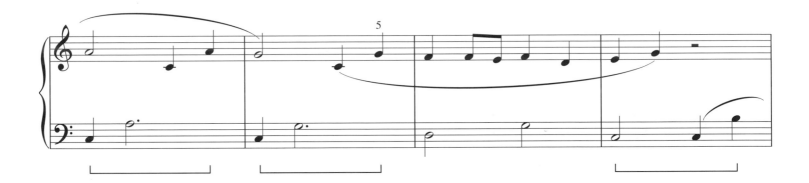

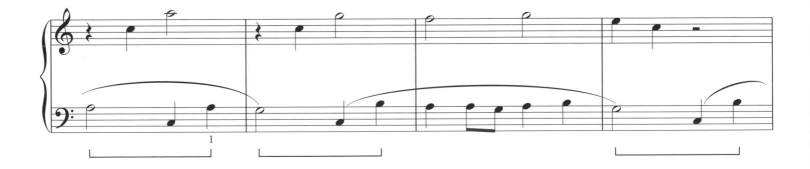

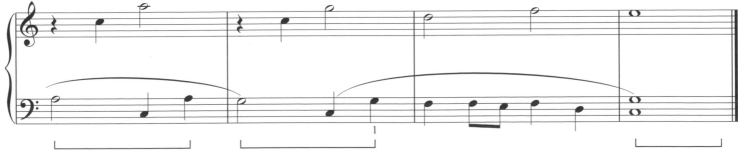

Unit 9: Octaves

Octave on the keyboard

Octaves on lines and spaces

The interval of an octave skips **six** white keys. On the staff, octaves skip **six** lines/spaces (three spaces and three lines), and go from a line note to a space note or from a space note to a line note.

What other intervals go from a line to a space and a space to a line? _____, _____, and _____

Exploring

Finding octaves on the keyboard is fun and simple. Play a G and then skip six white keys to go up an octave. What note did you end on? It should have been another G.

Using finger 2 of either hand, play the following puzzles. Begin on the note indicated and use the same finger to play up and down as indicated by the arrow and interval. Write the name of the last note on the line.

1. F ↑octave ↑2nd ↓3rd ↓octave ↓2nd ↑5th _____

2. A ↑3rd ↓octave ↑2nd ↑7th ↑2nd ↑3rd _____

3. B ↓4th ↓octave ↑3rd ↑6th ↓2nd _____

Circle the keyboards that show octaves.

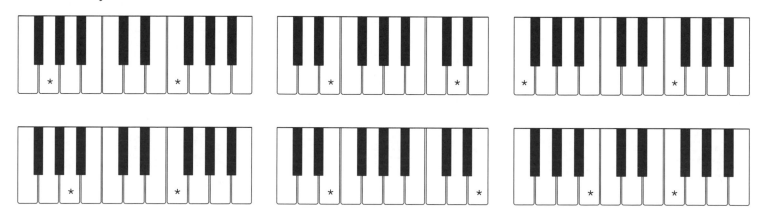

Draw an X **up** an octave from each named key on the keyboard.

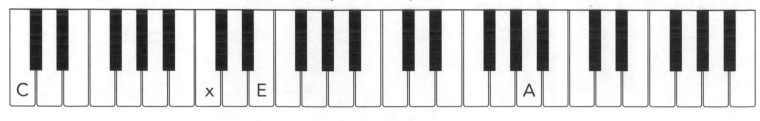

Draw an X **down** an octave from each named key on the keyboard.

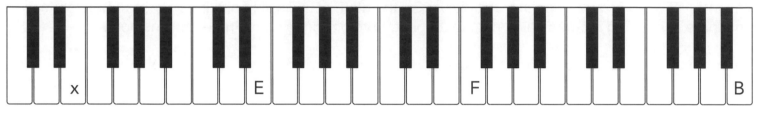

Writing

Circle the staves that show octaves.

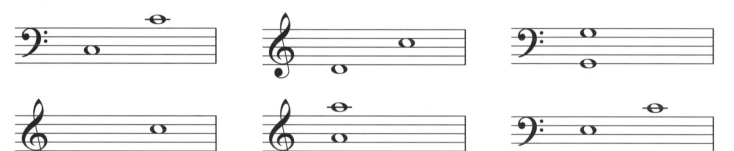

Draw the note **up** an octave from each of these notes.

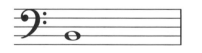

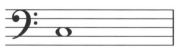

Draw the note **down** an octave from each of these notes.

Draw the notes going up and down as indicated by the arrows and intervals.

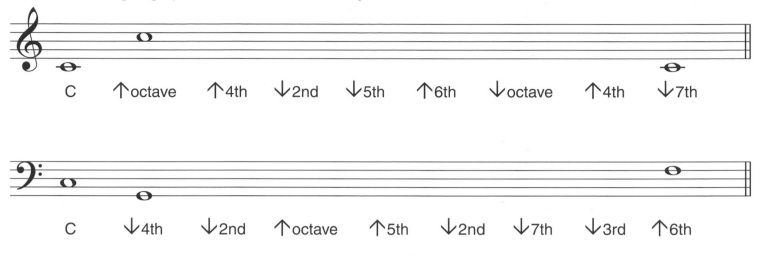

C   ↑octave   ↑4th   ↓2nd   ↓5th   ↑6th   ↓octave   ↑4th   ↓7th

C   ↓4th   ↓2nd   ↑octave   ↑5th   ↓2nd   ↓7th   ↓3rd   ↑6th

Playing

Playing an octave requires you to reach beyond a 7th. When you play an octave, keep your wrist relaxed.

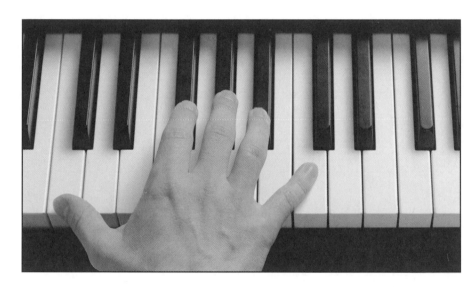

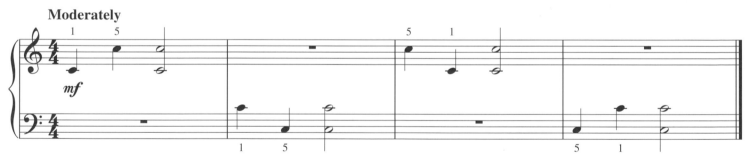

Play each puzzle first in your lap, then on the piano. Say the direction and interval as indicated while you play. Write the name of the last note in the blank.

1. Begin with LH finger 5 on C: C   ↑octave   ↓2nd   ↓4th   ↑6th   ↓2nd   ↓4th _____

2. Begin with RH finger 5 on G: G   ↓5th   ↑octave   ↓2nd   ↓4th   ↑7th   ↓3rd _____

Reading

For each example, place your hand in your lap or on the keyboard cover and play and say the direction and interval ("up an octave," "down a 4th," etc.).

Next, play the example on the keyboard and say the intervals again as you play.

1.

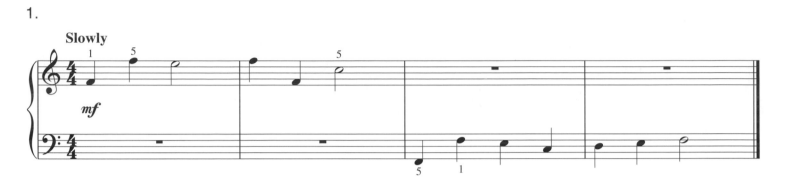

2.

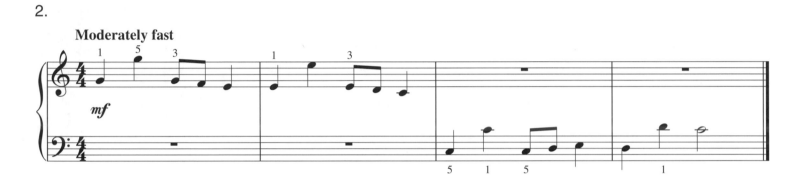

3.

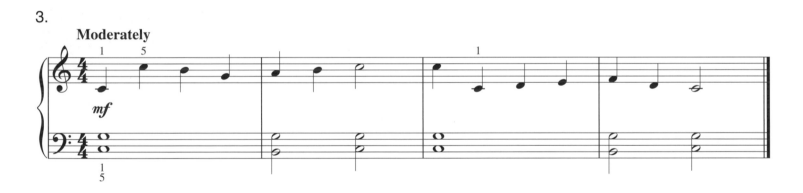

Creating

Explore the sound of octaves and make your own piece. Here is an idea to help you get started. Or just create your own!

Repertoire

Circle all the otaves in this piece. In line 3 the left hand plays harmonic intervals _____, _____, and _____, while the right hand plays harmonic _____.

Practice each line hands separately before playing hands together. To add the pedal, first practice the left hand alone with pedal, then hands together.

Sunrise Over the Mountains

By Craig Sale

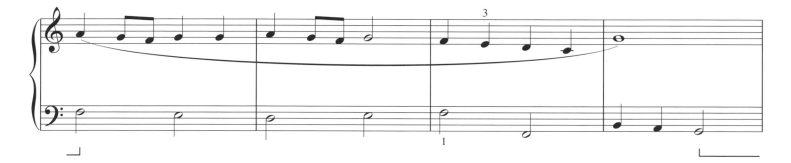

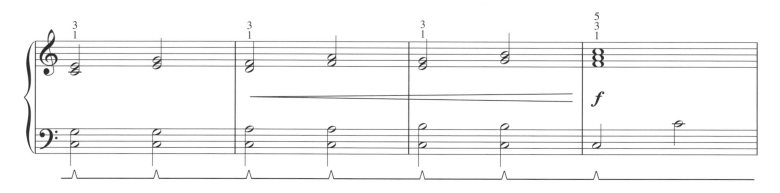

Unit 10: Interval Review

Exploring

On the keyboard below, go up or down, the designated interval from each X and write the name of that key. The first one is done for you.

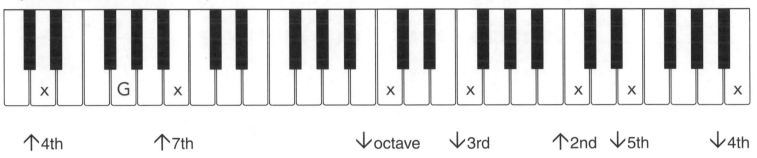

↑4th　　　　　↑7th　　　　　↓octave　↓3rd　　↑2nd ↓5th　　↓4th

Just use your mind to solve these interval puzzles—no fingers, no keys—just your brain!

1. THINK: F　↑4　↑octave　↓2　↓5　↑5　　　What note did you imagine ending on?　___

2. THINK: G　↓octave　↑7　↑3　↓2　↓5　↑3　　What note did you imagine ending on?　___

3. THINK: D　↑5　↑5　↓octave　↑3　↑6　　　What note did you imagine ending on?　___

Writing

Draw the interval **above** each note as indicated by the number. Then, write the name of the note you draw on the line.

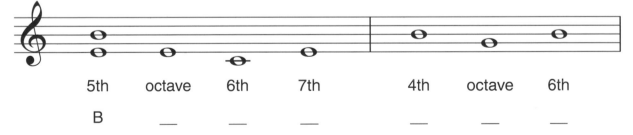

5th　　octave　　6th　　7th　　　4th　　octave　　6th

B　　___　　___　　___　　　___　　___　　___

Draw the interval **below** each note as indicated by the number. Then, write the name of the note you draw on the line.

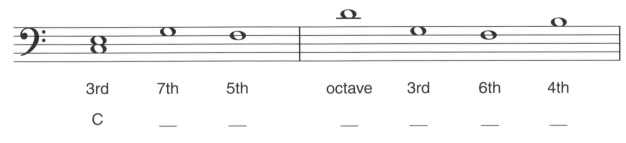

3rd　　7th　　5th　　　octave　　3rd　　6th　　4th

C　　___　　___　　　___　　___　　___　　___

Fill in the missing notes as indicated by the arrow and interval. Make sure you keep the correct number of beats in each measure. Then play the tune. Do you recognize it? Write the title on the line.

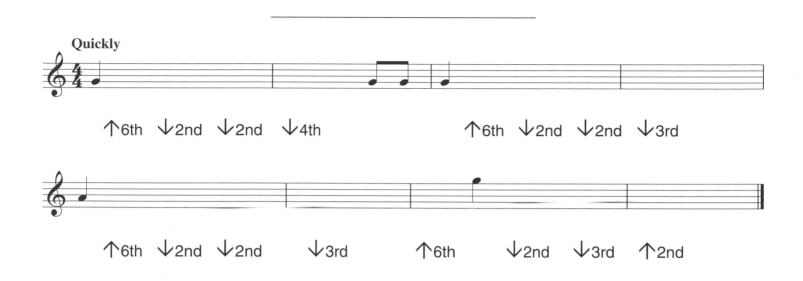

Quickly

↑6th ↓2nd ↓2nd ↓4th   ↑6th ↓2nd ↓2nd ↓3rd

↑6th ↓2nd ↓2nd   ↓3rd   ↑6th   ↓2nd   ↓3rd   ↑2nd

Playing and Writing

Play and say the direction and intervals, then write the notes on the staff. Play what you have written to be sure they match!

1. Begin with RH finger 1 on E:

E ↑7th ↓3rd ↑2nd ↓4th ↑6th ↓3rd

2. Begin with LH finger 5 on C:

C ↑3rd ↓2nd ↓2nd ↑octave ↓6th ↑2nd

Creating your own piece

Make your own piece using all of the intervals—2nds through octaves. Here is an idea to help you get started. Or just create your own!

Moderately fast

Before practicing "Amazing Grace," study the left-hand intervals. Practice each hand alone before playing hands together. Listen for a smooth right-hand melody.

Amazing Grace

American Hymn

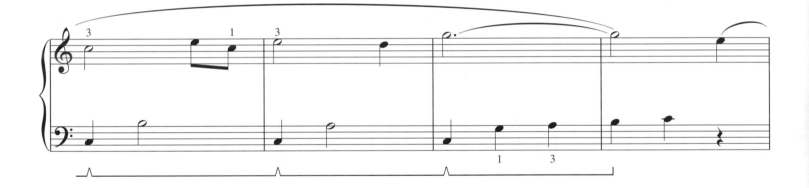

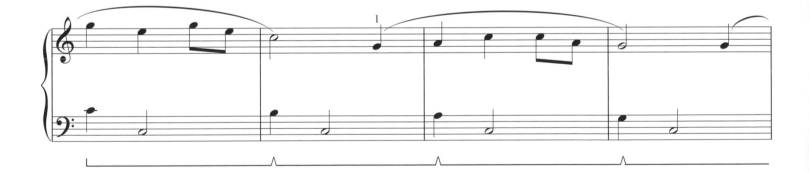